The One

*In the Search for My Husband,
I Found My FATHER*

Karen Mutchler Allen

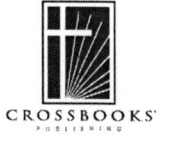

CROSSBOOKS

CrossBooks™
A Division of LifeWay
1663 Liberty Drive
Bloomington, IN 47403
www.crossbooks.com
Phone: 1-866-879-0502

©2010 Karen Mutchler Allen. All rights reserved.

No part of this book may be reproduced, stored in a retrieval system, or transmitted by any means without the written permission of the author.

First published by CrossBooks 11/12/2010

ISBN: 978-1-6150-7631-4 (sc)

Unless otherwise indicated, Bible quotations are taken from The NIV Study Bible. Copyright 1985 The Zondervan Corporation

Printed in the United States of America

This book is printed on acid-free paper.

Any people depicted in stock imagery provided by Thinkstock are models, and such images are being used for illustrative purposes only.

Certain stock imagery © Thinkstock.

Because of the dynamic nature of the Internet, any Web addresses or links contained in this book may have changed since publication and may no longer be valid. The views expressed in this work are solely those of the author and do not necessarily reflect the views of the publisher, and the publisher hereby disclaims any responsibility for them.

Dedicated to

My mom & dad – you two are my heroes.

Lindale, Ry, JoJo, and little man – you all are my heart.

Contents

Acknowledgments		ix
1.	One	1
2.	One What?	3
3.	It's a Jungle Out There…	5
4.	The One?	9
5.	Dear Diary	11
6.	My Very Own Romance Novel	17
7.	"What If…?"	23
8.	Soul to Soul	29
9.	The Ultimate Romance	33
10.	To Find "The One" You Have to be "The One"	37
11.	You're Worth the Wait	49
12.	The Past has Passed	53
13.	This is NOT the Last Chapter…	57

Acknowledgments

Not very many people knew that I was writing a book. Sometimes I didn't even know **I** was writing a book! However, when the book was finished, there were "the few" that I sought help from. I have a sincere gratefulness to these individual for their help, input, and honesty. These were the brave people who read my "rough, rough draft" and shared their thoughts concerning the book. Time is so valuable and I am indebted to them for their sacrifice. I am honored to consider these wonderful, special people, my friends. Lindsey Allen, Sarah Clark, Bowdie Jenkins, Marty McPherson, and Dr. Jessica Richardson. I would also like to extend a huge thanks to my friend, Emily Bryant, for her time and talent of editing "The One".

I would also like to acknowledge my partner-in-crime-at-the-time Catherine Scupin. Ecclesiastes 4:9-10 says, "Two are better than one, because they have a good return for their work. If one falls down, his friend can help him up. But pity the man who falls and has no one to help him up!" Catherine helped me up many times in this journey. More times than I could ever count. Her friendship, loyalty, and prayers are what sustained me thru my days. I'm forever grateful to the LORD for putting this special friend in my life. There are many memories of God's provision, promise, perfection, and maybe more than anything, laughter. Thank you, Catherine.

And to all those who may be represented in this book, I would like to say, "Thank You". For without you, the journey would have been… well…boring.

Every long lost dream led me to where you are
Others who broke my heart they were like Northern stars
Pointing me on my way into your loving arms
This much I know is true
That God blessed the broken road
That led me straight to you

Rascal Flats <u>God bless the broken road</u>

One

"A hard beginning maketh a good ending."
John Heywood

My first date was when I was fifteen. It was supposed to be sixteen but somehow my parents caved and let me go a few months early. His name was Will. We went to see a movie called *Misery*. What a great first date movie, huh? I wore a green sweater that made my eyes dance, my favorite jeans and brown boots. Funny, I don't remember what he wore. Did it really even matter? I do, however, distinctly remember the strong scent of Drakar Noir. It was the same cologne my brother Jeff wore. I remember it creeped me out because it was like I was on a date with my brother. That, my friend, would be a whole different book. So, here we have a movie called *Misery*, a brotherly smell, and my "first" first date. And so began my journey for finding "The One." I can honestly say that at times, it resembled the movie title of my very first date… *Misery*.

One What?

Neo: What did she tell you?
Morpheus: That I would find the One.

Everywhere you turn you hear this term: "The One". What does it really mean anyway? Neo was supposed to be "The One" in the movie *Matrix*. Was he "The One" for Trinity or "The One" to save the world from destruction? Or was he both? The reality TV show, *The Bachelorette*, has one gal trying to find her "One" out of thirty possible suitors; sad to say that most of the time the couples break up in the end. Geez, all that stress and dating for what? So what's the deal? Is there just one person for everyone in the world? What if you never find that person? What if you do find that person but don't know they're "The One" after all? Do you get a "do-over" or a time machine or something? I guarantee it is easier to find a gallon of your favorite Ben & Jerry's ice cream in the Sahara Desert than it is to find 'The One' <u>anywhere</u>.

Why did God make it so hard? Did He? Who is "The One" for me anyway? Does God really care about my search or is He just an observer in this cat and mouse game? Well, I don't know if I can philosophically answer all of those questions, however, I can tell you what I've experienced. These next chapters will hopefully provide insight for this difficult search. I hope you enjoy the ride - I know I did.

It's a Jungle Out There...

"I've been dating since I was fifteen. I'm exhausted. Where is he?
Kristen Davis

Can I get a witness? The dating scene is hard enough as it is but then you add the pressure of finding the one person in the whole universe who completes you and "a jungle" is a complete understatement.

What makes dating so hard? It could be that dating is portrayed so differently on the movies than in real life. Two beautiful people find each other, have everything in common, and then just soar into 'happily-ever-after'. Reality is so different, isn't it? From awkward moments to uncomfortable silence, expectations are diminished and feelings of inadequacy are realized. Women are worried that they don't look enough like a super-model on the date and men are worried that if they DON'T hold the door, she'll be offended, but if they DO hold the door, she'll cry "Women's lib!" Dating is not easy; it is serious business, however. This jungle is full of lions and tigers and bears ("oh my") and here we sit, right in the middle of it all. Maybe we are waiting for prince (or princess) charming to find us. Maybe we are just praying we don't choose a bear when we are supposed to pick a tiger as we consider which 'ONE' will suit us best. We're looking for love in the jungle…which is hard if you're a city girl!!

I didn't have a serious boyfriend until my senior year of high school and really, how 'serious' is that anyway? Pretty much the day we broke up I already had another guy lined up to date. I'm sure that sounds a bit harsh but sometimes reality **is** harsh. This pattern of "keeping a guy around" seemed to show up quite consistently in my dating life: I probably didn't go 24 hours without having a boyfriend. I liked the sound of being someone's 'girl' even if I really didn't like *that someone* all that much. Having a boyfriend was like having a purse: I didn't always *need* a purse, but it was nice to have around **just in case**. You know, **just in case** there was a party; or **just in case** your birthday was coming up; or **just in case** you felt lonely. They (purses and boyfriends) were a great accessory to most outfits. I always felt a sense of safety and security... until we would break up. Then I would just search to find another purse, I mean, another guy to make me feel accessorized.

Have I mentioned the types of guys I chose to date? I'd better not. More for my good than theirs I assure you. I seemed to pick guys that **I** had to pursue. By the way it really was meant to be the other way around (I don't care what the Women's Right Movement says). I never dated guys that would ever tell me I was wonderful, beautiful, or worthy of their best. Okay, I did date one, but he was so 'into' me I dropped him like a hot potato. Looking back I can recognize the complete stupidity and ignorance of that mindset: it makes me quite aware that I would have benefited from a session with Dr. Phil on his show as he discussed "Relationship Sabotage: Why you ruin a good thing". Regarding the not-so-nice guys I dated I remember asking one young man what he noticed about me on my prom night. Truth be known I was searching for a compliment. He said something to the effect of, "You looked okay. It made your butt look big." Does 'big' mean good? It better.

The majority of the guys I dated did not have a close personal relationship with the Lord or any relationship with Him at all for that matter. Whose fault was that? That would be mine. I chose to date them so what did I expect? I remember sitting at the kitchen table with my mom as we were talking about relationships. I was dating a guy who did not have a relationship with Christ and I knew that I shouldn't be dating him; at the time I didn't care. I told my mom in my best soap-opera style voice "Mom, you can't help who you fall in love with!" She answered, "You are right; you can't. That's why you'd better be sure he loves the Lord BEFORE you fall in love with him." Relationships without

The One

Christ lead to empty, unfulfilled, and miserable lives. The relationships I entered into that weren't Christ-centered were no exception.

I finally dated a guy who loved the Lord. There was just one itty bitty problem… Jon and I were great friends: no more, no less. We hung out; we laughed at the same movies, the same jokes, and each other. The relationship was actually really fun but I knew it wasn't quite right. I was so confused because I just figured that since he loved the Lord, he had to "The One" right? Wrong. Jon and I ended the relationship knowing it wasn't in God's plan for us to be together. However, I was finally on the right track of dating the right kind of guy. Or at least I hoped I was.

I was asked to chaperone a youth retreat and went along so I could "help" the youth grow and learn. What I did not expect was for God to show up and talk to ME! I remember sitting in the huge arena and listening to the speaker share the message of being "Sold Out" for Christ. He asked us to visualize our hearts as an auditorium with chairs filling each row. He then said to think about each chair as a specific area of our life: one chair could be our relationship with our parents; one chair could be our church life or our friends at school. The speaker then said something so profound that it resonated in my heart then just as powerfully as it does now. He said that if you were a Christian and claimed to be 'Sold Out' to Christ, then He should be sitting in each one of those chairs. If Christ wasn't then "you are not 'Sold Out' so don't claim to be." I swallowed hard and began to take a look at my chairs. Christ was sitting in my church life chair, my Quite-Time chair, my friendship chair and so on…but there was one that was empty. Yup, you guessed it: was my dating life chair. It was vacant. I realized on that youth retreat, the one **I** was supposed to be chaperoning, that God had just changed my life. First, He cared enough to tell me that I had an empty chair. Secondly, He loved me enough to re-direct my dating life in that very moment. I left that retreat a changed woman; I was completely 'Sold Out' and it felt wonderful. I couldn't wait to see how God was going to lead me now that my 'dating chair' was now occupied by my King.

It was shortly thereafter I began to see Dan. He was a guy who loved the Lord, and we had a lot in common. I think the main difference in this relationship was that it really was the first time in my life I actually gave the Lord my dating life. About time, huh? I kept asking the Lord to prepare my way and to give me direction in this relationship. God is so faithful: He showed me that His plan for me didn't include Dan. That's what happens when you seek Him in <u>all</u> things. I was asking Him for **His** plan and **His** best; I wanted what **HE** wanted for me. He didn't shout in a booming voice, "Dan's not the right guy!" nor did He write it on a billboard sign. But, because I had given Him my dating life, I was keenly aware of His approval. I did not have a peace to continue with the relationship: I just knew in my spirit that God was re-directing me. I was so grateful that the Lord saw fit to guide my decision. Still when it was time to make the decision to end the relationship and follow God's direction I was very nervous: you see the next step had not been revealed yet. We all know how difficult it is to walk when blindfolded. I had to trust that the One who was leading me was truly capable of leading the blind.

Then, I found him…

The One?

"Hope deferred makes the heart sick, but a longing fulfilled is the tree of life.
Proverbs 13:12

…or so I thought. Matthew was a godly man who was handsome and so in love with….the Lord. I bet you thought I was going to say 'me' huh? That's what I would have preferred at the time too, but that was certainly not the reality.

Matthew and I dated for two and a half years. He was all I had ever hoped for in a man. We were best friends and we enjoyed our time together; still something just wasn't right. He liked me-maybe even loved me: he just wasn't **in love** with me. He appreciated my presence but he didn't long for it. There is a difference. I began to see my world changing. It was falling apart around me and I didn't like it one bit.

Matthew and I eventually broke up and I was completely devastated. I can remember hearing about people breaking up and having such a hard time; I would sometimes think, "Good grief, just get over it already; put on your big girl panties and deal with it." But for the first time I felt broken and rejected. I didn't tell anyone at the school I taught at for over a month because if I mentioned it I would cry. I was a kindergarten teacher at the time and I can assure you five year old kids don't like when their teacher cries. I remember one day, shortly after the break up, getting into bed with all my clothes on and it was

5:00 pm. The only reason I got out of bed was because my best friend, Catherine, was on her way to comfort me with a bag of Starburst and a gallon of ice cream. I had to get out of bed and open the door...I could not, under any circumstance, let the ice cream melt.

I couldn't put my finger on just why I was so messed up over this: you know, why I couldn't put on those big girl panties? Then one day I was listening to one of my favorite worship leaders Dennis Jernigan and he summed up my feelings in one statement: he said, "Some of you have experienced a death of a vision." There it was. It took the breath out of me. He had hit the nail on the head. I had a death of a vision, a death of a dream. What I thought my life held, it did not. What I thought my future looked like, it no longer did: no wedding, no children, no happily-ever-after - at least not with Matthew anyway. Joseph Cambell wrote, "We must let go of the life we planned, so as to accept the one that is waiting for us." I didn't think I could do that. In fact I feared that the death of that vision would be the very death of me.

So I began a different journey. This new journey did not include a search for my husband. It was a search for my Heavenly Father. It was a search for strength, hope, healing, and unconditional love. I knew that there was only one who could fulfill me - "The ONE".

Dear Diary

"...write down the revelation and make it plain on tables so that a herald may run with it. For the revelation awaits an appointed time; it speaks of the end and will not prove false. Though it linger, wait for it; it will certainly come and will not delay."
Habakkuk 2:2-3

During this time of my life I kept a journal of time spent healing and trying to learn what God was teaching me. I can assure you of one thing: any time you go through something you can't handle on your own, God is going to teach you something. My mom, who rocks by the way, says that God never wastes a hurt. He doesn't. He can't. He's too in love with you.

These entries are intimate revelations into my world at the time. If you had asked me then if I would have shared them with the world, I would have laughed, made sure the journals were safe, sealed in a fireproof vault that was hidden in a shallow grave in the backyard, and then laughed again. But, God is faithful, so faithful. I desire for you to get just a glimpse of how my Abba healed, supported, listened, and answered during some of the most difficult and trying times in my life.

March 2, 1999

I can say that I have a passion for Christ - it has been revealed through suffering. This suffering is bringing forth perseverance and strength. It has also brought forth an insatiable hunger for the righteous things of God. I am seeking earnestly so I know I will find and I will lack no good thing. I continue to press on toward the goal to win the prize. The joy of the Lord is my strength. I believe that God will make all grace abound to me. I also know that while I continue to heal from a broken heart and shattered dreams, the God of Comfort offers His lap for me to sit on, His shoulder for me to rest and cry, and His strong arms to hold me securely. My Jehovah Jirah, God, my life and provider. It has been almost two months since we've broken up and a month since we've spoken. At times I feel strong and others I feel weak. I still wait for his call and look for his car in my driveway to deliver some good news only to be disappointed again.

March 6, 1999

My soul waits in silence for God only; from Him is my salvation." Psalm 62:1 This waiting requires faith, patience, constant prayer, discipline, and an expectancy that God will answer as He promised. Lord, I'm trusting you to handle this in your perfect way. You know my every need and my every fear and I'm trusting that whatever you decide - and whenever you decide it - is best. Thank you.

March 8, 1999

"But I trust in you O Lord; I say you are my God. My times are in your hands." Psalm 31:15 "Be strong and take heart all you who hope in the Lord" Psalm 15:24 ...Am I fighting a losing battle? Is there anything for me there? Am I the "One" or not? Could I have been at one time or so he thought? What changed - who changed? To top it all off one of my ex-boyfriends is engaged. Lord, you know that I'm glad it's not me but it actually feels weird. Every man I've had a serious relationship with says, "If I don't marry you I won't marry." They marry; I don't. You know that this isn't just about marriage. I know that I could be married right now - I just get frustrated sometimes. Waiting for You and for him. Lots of

waiting. I am called to so much more than just a marriage. I know that. I feel like I need to fight only I have to do it in silence. How? My hope rests in You. Remind me that You are my only certain future. I will rejoice with thanksgiving.

April 18, 1999

...Lord, I understand and recognize my complete need for you. My dependency is on You and You alone because You are the only one able to be perfect in this. These three months have been a time for me to learn to depend, lean, and totally trust You. You are my life.

I saw him again and again I was heartbroken. Even just the sight of him reminded me of what I thought I had lost. Of what I still wanted even though I knew that the Lord had moved us both in different directions. I felt hurt all over again: two steps forward, a million steps back.

May 25, 1999

"When you pass thru the waters I will be with you and when you pass thru the rivers they will not sweep over you. When you walk thru the fire you will not be burned, the flames will not set you ablaze. For I am the Lord your God, the Holy One of Israel, your Savior." Isaiah 43:2-3 I am not alone.

June 28, 1999

"The eyes of all look to you and you give them their food at the proper time. You open your hand and satisfy the desires of every living thing." Psalm 145:15-16

My eyes are fixed on You, O Lord, knowing that at the proper time You will open Your hand and feed me the desires of my heart. Thank You for Your sweet, gentle reminders. "The Lord is faithful to all his promises" vs. 13. You have promised me the richest blessings and the ultimate best for my life. Let me never get caught up in what I do not have now as to cloud the hope of what is to come - my perfect husband.

This next journal entry really was a huge moment for me. God showed me what I didn't even know I was missing. I love when He does that. This Word from the Lord was such an encouragement to me because it really focused me as I began looking forward to my future once again.

July 6th 1999

"Delight yourself in the Lord and he will give you the desires of your heart." Psalm 37:4 …God asked me to go back to Psalm 37:4 and tell Him what the desires of my heart were. I realized that that was the problem. I didn't truly know what those desires were. He had me write them down and they came to just three things: to marry a godly man soon, to have his children, and to speak God's Word to youth and young adults. God said, "Look over it and tell me what you see." I noticed that they were simple; I noticed that they were somewhat different than before, and then I noticed what God needed me to see - the word 'soon.' I desire God's man soon. Had I not written it all out I would not have realized that was my desire. The Lord desires for our desires to match His, and He has confirmed that these do. My desire is for my husband to come soon. I know you, Lord, I know he's coming soon, whoever he is. I can hardly wait to see this man.

This opened my world up to dating again. I was a little reluctant to head back in the same jungle that swallowed me whole not so long ago, but I knew that this time, there would be a different outcome. This time, I would be leaving the jungle with my prince charming and there would be no monkeys allowed!

Months and months had passed, but time wasn't what I was counting. I was counting on the goodness of my Father in Heaven to deliver me His best.

Here is a journal entry after my very first date in over two-and-a-half years.

July 11, 1999

"Whether you turn to the right or left, your ears will hear a voice behind you saying, "This is the way; walk in it." Isaiah 30:21 You were faithful yet again, Lord, in telling me the way to walk. This

guy I went on a date with is not my husband and I thank you for allowing me to know right away. At first I wondered why You had me go on this date when You knew he wasn't mine and then you said, "You had to be able to recognize when he wasn't yours so you will be able to recognize when he (your husband) is." Thank You also for reminding me that I'm okay: guys find me interesting, fun, and want to spend time with me. Thank You that the words that flowed through my mouth were words about You. My passion for You came through like a mighty rushing wind. There was no doubt in this guy's mind who I belonged to and where my heart was. You have made me strong in that - thank You. I know that in order for You to fulfill the word 'soon' I must go on a date or two! Continue to bring me the strength to say yes as You send my husband soon. I am amazed by Your goodness, Oh Lord.

In my search for my husband, I found my FATHER

August 3, 1999

"It was good for me to be afflicted so that I might learn your decrees." Psalm 119:71 How this rings true in my life! It really was good for me to be afflicted. To feel so completely heart-broken and helpless was the only place to be because I realized the one and only constant in my life: because of the breakup I fell back in love with my First Love. I rediscovered Him in such a new way. I started spending time with Him: I began truly desiring to know Him. I began searching in His Word and learning His decrees. If I had never gone through this thing, I would have never ran to my Savior, to the Lord who gives me breath. I would have never completely realized my dependency on Him. Over time I have seen why God chose to do what He did: He knew that I would never lean totally on Him, desire to study His Word, be bold and passionate, or be worthy of the calling to speak if I had stayed with Matthew. I was content where I was which makes God uncomfortable. In order for me to have moved ahead God had to throw off every hindrance that would bind me. Because of the freedom that God so richly gave me, I have climbed upon His wings and have soared. In this constant state of persevering I wait expectantly; it will finish its work in me and I will be mature and fully complete, lacking nothing. What a road! This journey has been

tough and even brutal, but I know in full confidence that it is for His glory I had to be afflicted or I would have never recognized God's calling or His goodness in fulfilling promises or His decrees. Without affliction I would be nothing.

Well, well, well what have we here? That doesn't sound like the chic who wasn't happy unless she had a purse to match her outfit, huh? What happened to the girl who needed a boyfriend to feel secure? What happened to the girl who liked being someone's 'girl'? What happened to the girl who always had a backup boyfriend? That girl found her Man in Jesus Christ and in *His* sufficiency. *That's* what happened to that girl. Praise the Lord!

My Very Own Romance Novel

In the silence of night I have often wished for just a few words of love from one man, rather than the applause of thousands of people
Judy Garland

I spent almost nine months nurturing my relationship with my Heavenly Father. Then, something happened, something I didn't expect. My very own romance novel began to unfold right before my very eyes.

My brother Jeff was getting married and we were all set for the rehearsal dinner. I walked into the church and there stood a man. I looked at this man and the Lord spoke to my spirit and said, "There is your husband." The first thing I thought was, "God, you did good!" because he was unbelievably handsome. Then I thought, "Did He just say what I thought He said?" The rest of the evening was spent talking to this gentleman. His name was Lindsey Allen and he and my brother had been roommates for six months. I remember meeting him briefly in May at a huge church crusade. At the time, I was still healing and had no interest in dating so even if he had asked me out then my answer would have been a polite "no thank you." I even leaned over to Catherine and said, "Hey, that Lindsey guy would make a great husband for you!" Really glad she didn't take me up on that advice!!

I found out from Lindsey later that he had seen a picture of me and asked Jeff to set us up. Jeff adamantly refused for Lindsey's sake, saying something to the effect of "You don't want to go out with her! She's hard-headed and really stubborn!" I think that's called brotherly love or maybe it's just a typical brotherly answer. Either way it deterred Lindsey from asking me out for the time being. Thank you oh brother of mine! As far as Lindsey knew I was a crazy, determined, head strong, stubborn girl. He might have been right! However, now the time was right and the Lord had set His plan in motion.

So here we are at the rehearsal dinner; we spent the night of the dinner talking to each other. It was like no one else was in the room. My dad even commented later that the chemistry was undeniable. I can honestly say that I had never experienced anything like this before. Carl Gustav Jung says, "The meeting of two personalities is like the contact of two chemical substances; if there is any reaction, both are transformed." And let me tell you, there was certainly a reaction!

He was a teacher, just as I was. Of course I found that to be irresistible! He loved my Lord which I found even more irresistible. I was shaken in my boots for sure! I got into my car to go home that night and I was in awe. Not in awe of the man I had just met, but in awe of God's faithfulness in my life. When I got home, I made a phone call to my best friend Catherine who had been traveling this journey so faithfully with me. I said, "Hey, I met my husband tonight". Her response was quite typical of her, "Well, praise the Lord!"

I sat down and the Lord revealed even more of his heart to me that night in His Word. This is my journal entry that night: the night I met "The One".

September 3, 1999

"I have found David, son of Jesse, a man after my own heart, he will do everything I want him to do." Acts 13:23b

How amazing! Tonight at the rehearsal dinner I met my husband. His name is Lindsey Allen. I know in my spirit; I recognized him. He has just broken up with his girlfriend because God said to. He also talked about his classroom and how that's where God wants his ministry - a man who is asking, listening and obeying. A man after God's own heart. God has spoken "he will do everything I want him to do". Lindsey will listen and obey. I stand firm on that promise. Lindsey has a ministry - his class; he is a minister!! He has all that is needed to stir me. I am attracted to him physically and spiritually - completely satisfied. Never have I been so sure of what God has spoken - he is your husband. I love him completely because I know he's God's mate for my life. Since the day I asked the Lord to allow me to recognize my husband I had yet to do so. Now I know - I also know I have no idea what he feels toward me or even if he likes me. I do however, trust him spiritually enough to know that when God speaks he will listen and act. Abba, you are amazing, simply amazing. I asked you to allow me to recognize my husband - You did. I wasn't exactly sure how I would know but I just do. Thank You for Your faithfulness in my life. Thank You for my husband. I know you have been preparing him; he wasn't ready in May when I met him. You kept telling me to "just hang on; I'm not finished with him yet." Complete. Complete in You...complete for each other. Perseverance must finish its work so you may be mature and fully compete, lacking nothing. You have healed my heart through perseverance and now I'm complete and ready for Lindsey. Give him boldness Lord to capture me - only, he already has. Give us wisdom and Your timing because obviously it's perfect. Thank You for my husband. Bless him beyond measure because you've already done it for me. Amazing.

We were married seven months later. You read it right...seven months. Everything was perfect, especially my wedding dress. It too has a story. Lindsey and I started dating in September. One day in November I was sitting at my desk at school and the Lord spoke to me: He said the funniest thing, "Go buy your wedding dress." Yep! That's what I did too: raised my eyebrows and laughed just like you just did. As funny as this was there was no denying His strange request. I called my partner in crime, Catherine, and that day we went shopping for a dress - one that was white and full of meaning...a wedding dress.

I found it - you know, "The One". It was perfect. Finding your wedding dress is like finding your favorite haircut; it looks great on you but it's not necessarily how you look in it: it's how you **feel** you look in it. I called my mom and here's how the conversation went:

Me: "Mom, would you mind coming down here and paying for my wedding dress?"

There was a pause on the other end of the phone.
Mom: "Um, are you engaged?"
"No", I said.
A simple question followed by an even simpler answer.
Mom: "Is there a promise of an engagement?"
Karen: "Not yet."

Understanding her confusion I explained to her that the Lord had prompted this buying experience. Being the godly woman that my mom is, she agreed and graciously bought my perfect wedding dress. She did however, ask me not to say anything to my dad until she explained it all to him. Fathers apparently don't like to buy wedding dresses for their daughters just for the heck of it…who knew?

In case you don't know, it typically takes about three months for a wedding dress to be ordered, shipped, and to arrive at the store. Then there are alterations to be made. Lindsey and I were married three months to the day that he proposed so I wouldn't have been able to have that particularly perfect wedding dress. God allowed me to have His best even in a wedding dress.

And just to add to the humor of this story, (as if it didn't have enough already) I knew I had to tell Lindsey that I had bought my gown on that November day since I didn't want him hearing it from anyone else. His friends told him to run and run fast when they heard about it; I'm sure glad he didn't decide to run. Remember we had only been dating for about two months at the time of my dress buying experience. He and I were on a date eating at a Mexican restaurant when I told him about the dress. He started sweating profusely. He said it was the salsa…I knew better. It was the salsa AND the thought of a certain white dress.

We were married April 1st, 2000. Yes, April Fools Day. It was spring break for the both of us and a perfect time to get married and go on our honeymoon. I often joked that if our anniversary was on April Fool's Day and Lindsey forgot, he could always say, "Just kidding babe, April Fools!" (He NEVER has though; he's a good man!!) There was no joking about this marriage. It was the real deal because it had been ordained by the King of Kings and the Lord of Lords. Here is my journal entry the morning of my wedding day.

April 1, 2000

"All night long on my bed I looked for the one my heart loves; I looked for him but did not find him." Song of Songs 3:1. I sit here on the morning of my wedding day remembering when I was a "Lady in Waiting" just like Esther. She was a Lady in Waiting for twelve months in order to be presented to the King. If she found favor with him, he would summon her by name. The Lord took me through a time such as this. Months and months went into preparing my mind, heart and spirit so that when I met my king he would find favor with me. Today, God's man will call me by name. To an extent I am still a Lady in Waiting. I am waiting to see God's richest and abundant blessings be poured out in the land of the living. I no longer must wait for my earthly bridegroom – just my heavenly one. My ultimate prayer for my wedding day is that the God who so awesomely joined us will be magnified and glorified. May the presence of Jehovah fill the sanctuary with power, joy, and hope. The time has come when the completion of God's promises come into full view: His plan has been revealed and carried out. Heartaches, heartbreaks, and pain are revealed for what they are.: the means to an end. The catalyst for focusing on and completely depending on Christ, the author and perfector of our faith. The Master Author has written His ultimate earthly love story as told in the lives of Lindsey and me. Thank You, Jesus.

It's funny: when I stopped looking for a husband, I found him. I thought I had begun the search for <u>the one</u> relationship that would complete me. <u>The one</u> relationship that would never reject me or hurt me. I was seeking <u>the one</u> relationship in my life that I couldn't live without. Jeremiah 29:13 says, "You will seek me and find me when you seek me with all your heart." I recognized the need I had for an intimate relationship with the Lord, not a Sunday-only-talk-to-Him-when-I-need-something kind of relationship. He was my Portion, my Creator, my Healer, my Friend. I had more of a need for Him than I did any man.

Have you been so busy looking for your mate that you've neglected your Maker? Have you spent more time dreaming about being engaged that you haven't been engaging in a relationship with the Lord? Have you been searching for intimacy in a lasting relationship but you've missed the intimate love relationship that Christ longs to give you? You are not alone. I wasn't either.

The Lord longed to make me whole. He wanted to be my all-in-all, my best friend. He was the Lover of my soul. When I embraced the Lord He embraced me back. It was such an enlightening time for me. Remember Psalm 119:71? It says, "It was good for me to be afflicted so I might learn your decrees." His decrees are His Word. God's Word reflects His heart. When you know God's heart you know God.

I'm not saying that if you have an intimate relationship with Christ He'll be sending your mate soon. I'm just saying that it's the best place to be in order for God to work on YOU. Stay focused on the prize. And by the way, the prize isn't a mate: it's the opportunity to love and to be loved by God Himself.

"What If...?"

It's in your moments of decision that your destiny is shaped.
Anthony Robbins

"What if I'm not like you?" you might ask. Well consider yourself really lucky! Just kidding! Many of you may have read the last few chapters and started freaking out: questions swirl through your mind such as, "What if my story doesn't happen like that?" or maybe, "What if I never find "The One"? Will I forever be miserable?" You might even be asking, "Is there really such thing as a soul-mate?" These are all legitimate questions and concerns, and trust me, I hear ya!

First, know that every story is written differently: no two stories will be exactly alike. In fact if all of our 'found him/her' stories were alike there would be no reason to share them. I also think that if *my* story was the same as everyone else's it wouldn't be, well…as miraculous, as I think it is. It wouldn't point to God as much as I'd hoped if we all found our special "someone' the same way.

So allow your story to be different. However God has ordained your meeting with your mate is EXACTLY how it needs to be. My story (**all stories** for that matter) is used to encourage your journey not dictate it. I think that the most important concept to remember is that you need to be ready, willing, and open to what God desires for you in the realm of dating and marriage.

What I have found is that for some people dating has never been a spiritual decision; therefore their choice of mate has never been a spiritual one either. I don't mean this in a negative or derogatory sense; it's just that some people have never even known to ask the Lord for direction in dating and marriage. My best advice to anyone is to be sure that your dating journey is guided by the Lord. I've been asked a million times, "How did you **KNOW** Lindsey was "The One"? I know it sounds peculiar for me to say, "Well, the LORD told me!" Except… the LORD **really** did tell me. He may not do that for you. Or, He may. I hope to give you some ways that the Lord can speak to you in order to give you direction, not just in dating, but life in general. God speaks to us specifically in three ways: through His Word, through prayer, and through other people.

Have you ever read someone else's mail? You don't have to answer that out loud if you don't want to: just nod your head slightly. Okay great: me too. What does reading someone else's mail do for you (besides make you feel a little guilty)? It gives insight on who they are, right? It is like a sneak peak into their life, a portal into their soul. Well maybe not a portal but you get the idea. Someone else's mail is a pretty good indicator of who they are, who their friends are, what is important to them, or what makes them tick. I can only imagine that if you decided to read someone else's mail everyday for a whole month you would learn much about them. I would guess that you would have a pretty good idea what kind of person he or she is. Actually it's a comforting thought while you are sitting in jail for stealing other people's mail, but at least you'll have plenty of reading material!

God's Word, the Bible, is a compilation of letters to us from God Himself. The Bible is full of real-life application with amazing people who are great examples of wise and not-so-wise choices. I believe that the Bible was created by God to help those of us who are learning to hear: not physical hearing, mind you, but spiritual hearing. It's for those of us who are growing in our ability to hear and know His voice; it's for those of us who 'need to see it to believe it'. The Bible is the written Word of God's heart. You want to know God? Then get to know His Word. He speaks through His Word. Every book, chapter, and verse originates from our Creator's very heart. So often I hear, "I just don't know what God wants me to do?" My answer is always the same: "Have you taken

The One

it to the Word?" What I mean is have you taken your question to the Scripture? That is the very place that God could use to answer and give you direction.

There is a verse for EVERY situation that comes about in our lives. You may find that hard to believe, but I can assure you there is! Even if the Bible does not address a specific situation, it does address how to go about handling everything…that, in turn, will bring you an answer. For instance, maybe you are trying to figure out how to handle a situation at work with an arrogant, degrading, mean boss: 1 Thessalonians 5:12 says, "…respect those who work hard among you, who are over you in the Lord, and who admonish you. Hold them in the highest regard in love because of their work. Live in peace with each other. And we urge you, brothers, warn those who are idle, encourage the timid, help the weak, be patient with everyone…but always try to be kind to each other and to everyone else." I never said it would be easy advice, just the right advice!!

Maybe you are trying to decide on a certain someone to date. Let's just say that you've been out a few times for fun and now it's getting to the point where it begins to be a little more serious. On the last date you talked 'religion' with him or her and found out that they don't know Christ. Now, you, being the person who has learned to make every decision a spiritual one, need to decide if you will continue to date this person or not. Guess what? There's a verse in the Bible for that too! Yep! 2 Corinthians 6:14 says, "Do not be yoked together with unbelievers. For what do righteousness and wickedness have in common? Or what fellowship can light have with darkness?"

What I'm trying to share with you is this: God speaks to us through His Word. He uses the Scriptures to reveal to our hearts, "Yes, this is what I want you to know". The thing is, the more you get to know God's Word, the more you get to know the person of God. There are so many times in my life that I have needed to hear from God and because I've spent a long time investing in and knowing who He is, I KNOW what He wants to tell me. I KNOW His heart for me. I KNOW the next step because I know God's heart. Looking in His Word is an important way to know Him and to hear what He is telling you. I encourage you to 'take it to the Word' anytime you need direction. Sit in a quiet place with your Bible. Ask the LORD to speak to you through His holy Word. Ask Him to impress upon your heart and mind a place to start reading, a word to get you started, or possibly a book of the Bible to begin with. Close your eyes and listen, really listen. You will hear a whisper brush over you. Maybe it's a specific word that you hear so you can look it up in the concordance in the back of your Bible. Scan the list of verses in the concordance and read any or all of the verses there. When you get to the one He wants you to read it will seem to jump of the page to you. It will capture your attention, making you read it again and thanking Him for his direction.

Maybe you don't hear a specific word but instead you hear a book of the Bible. Open your Bible and begin to scan the titles of each chapter or section in that particular book. See if one of them leaps off the page at you. Search until you find what you need or until He leads you in another direction. God may give you the book, chapter, and verse. When He does that, I literally do a little 'Jesus dance' wherever I am because that just ROCKS!!! He WILL speak through His Word: we just have to be ready to do some of the looking!

Not only does God speak and direct us through His Word He also speaks to us through prayer. Some people freak out when they think about praying, but really prayer is so simple. It is communicating with God. You talk; He listens. He talks; you listen. It really is that easy. We've made prayer harder than what it is. Prayers are conversations with your Daddy; that's all. As you pray and share your heart with God He hears you and He will answer you. Jeremiah 29:12 says, "Then you will call upon me and come and pray to me and I will listen to you." Prayer is a powerful way to find direction from the Lord. People have asked me, "Karen, do you actually 'hear' God speak?" For me, the answer is yes: I do hear His voice. It's not the booming 'God voice' you hear on TV but I do hear His voice nonetheless. In John 10:27, Jesus says, "My sheep listen to my voice; I know them, and they follow me." I truly believe that as you grow in your relationship with the Lord you too will 'hear' Him. There's not a day that goes by where I don't hear Him speak to me. A piece of me would die if He didn't. I need to hear His voice because I need direction for my life: I need Him. 1 Thessalonians 5:17 says, "Pray without ceasing". To me that is an all day long event: talking, listening, communing with my Savior. Prayer is an avenue in which God speaks to His children. So, pray…and pray often.

The last way I think the Lord speaks to us is through other people: God uses other people to help guide us in our decision making. It's called 'wise counsel' and it's something I hope you get used to seeking. Proverbs 15:22 says, "Plans fail for lack of counsel, but with many advisers they succeed." We don't know it all; some may think they do, but they don't. Sometimes we need help from others but not just 'any' help: help from those who are wise in the Lord. When you have a decision to make and need wise counsel to help your direction choose someone you trust. Choose someone who you think has a strong relationship with Christ and will give you wise counsel. Proverbs 27:17 shares, "As iron sharpens iron, so one man sharpens another." When we need help Godly counsel is there to sharpen us. It is okay to ask for advice and counsel from someone you consider wise. In fact the Old Testament is full of people that sought Godly counsel from someone God used as His very own mouthpiece. Some of you may ask, "But how do I know that this person is telling me is right? How do I know this is what God wants me to do?" I am a firm believer that God will never contradict His Word – He can't. So after I get a word from someone giving me counsel, I go straight to His Word to check it out. God always confirms what is said with what is in His Word. I can't tell you how many times people have come to me and asked "Here's my problem. What do you think I should do?" I pray about their problem, seek His voice, and then I share what God has laid on my heart for them. I am the asker as often as the giver: there have been times that I have had huge decisions to make and I go to the few people I trust to help with my decision-making and ask, "I need your wisdom – can you help me?" The President of the United States has an advisory board, one who helps him with any major decisions he has to make on our behalf. It is common practice to seek help and advice when you are not sure of what decision to make; it shouldn't be any different whether you are the President of the United States or a stay-at-home mom from Georgia.

Soul to Soul

Whatever our souls are made of, his and mine are the same.
Emily Bronte

I am often asked, "What if there are no such things as soul mates? What if soul mates do exist and I can't find mine?" I have thought, "What if my soul mate lives in China? I won't EVER have enough frequent flyer miles to get to China, not to mention I'm really attracted to sandy blonde headed guys who are 5'10 and taller." I would like to share my thoughts on the 'soul mate' phenomenon. Please remember that I'm only giving my perspective on this idea so if it differs from yours that is okay. No harm, no foul. An opinion is like a nose: everyone has one some are just bigger than others!

The definition of 'soul' can be described as person's emotional and moral nature, where the most private thoughts and feelings are hidden. Some synonyms for 'soul' are spirit, essence, **heart**, core, and character. The definition of 'mate' that is fitting is described as something that **matches** or **belongs together**. If I were to put these definitions together using the key words just listed it would be something to the effect of 'two matching hearts' or 'two characters that match'. When you dissect 'soul mates' it is not as mythical and magical as it may have once appeared. It doesn't seem like it is a cataclysmic collision of fate so much as a choice: it is a decision to find someone who matches your heart. How is that done? It is done by choosing someone who, at the core of their essence, is similar to you. By similar I mean in values, in morals, in ideas, in goals, and in purpose. We are all created differently and for good reason. Choosing a person who 'matches your heart' is not about choosing a clone of yourself or trying to find someone who likes *exactly* the same things you do; it's recognizing the depth of a person and appreciating who they are, and who they can be in your own life.

Biblically the idea of 'soul mates' is not specifically addressed, but as I've looked through the Scriptures I have found some interesting stories that have led me to my hypothesis concerning 'soul mates'.

I think that Solomon just may take the cake when it comes to marriages. In 1 Kings 11 it tells us that he had seven hundred wives and three hundred concubines. Lindsey told me once after reading this, "I can't keep up with the wife I have; why in the world would I want more?" Good question. Solomon obviously did not see the need for a soul mate; he did not feel that he needed just ONE person to match his heart or character. I'm sure that out of those one thousand 'loves of his life' there was someone who could have been his match but I don't know if he would have remembered finding her since there was so many. Can you imagine having all those women in one room? Can you imagine the drama? You know, for being the wisest man in the world he sure was kind of stupid, huh?

Solomon's father, King David, is another example of why I don't believe that soul mates are all what they seem. Eight wives were named in the Bible, but there were numerous other wives that were not named: Ahinoam the Jezreelitess, Abilgail the Carmelitess, Maachah the daughter of Talmai king of Geshur, Haggith, Abital, Eglah, Michal, and Bathsua the daughter of Ammiel. Now granted back in the Old Testament times marriages were viewed quite differently. In the New Testament 1Timothy 3:2 reminds us that an overseer or deacon must be the husband of but one wife so obviously the Lord is not teaching polygamy.

The important thing to remember here is that we want to find the person who is the other half of our 'two matching hearts' or 'two characters that match'. I think that it is a mistake to believe that there is only **one** person in the entire universe that you could share your heart and life with. In contemplating this idea, I often think, "If there really is only one person in the whole for me and that person is Lindsey, what would happen if he died?" Is that it for me and my happiness? Do I marry again knowing that my new husband would not be my soul mate?

It is my belief that there are *characteristics* that we are looking for in our search for "The One". We look for values and morals that match ours. We look for compatible personalities that we find attractive. We desire to be with someone who we find physically attractive as well. If you think about all of those criteria it's a little hard to believe that only ONE person in the **entire** world would fit those criteria.

Do I think I married the person God intended for me to marry? Absolutely. I married someone who matches my character and who matches my heart. He matches my heart for the Lord, for godliness, morality, and values. That is what makes him my soul mate. I asked my dad what he thought about soul mates and he said, "I think the person you marry <u>becomes</u> your soul mate." I think that is well-stated; the person you choose becomes your soul mate because they DO match your soul or your essence.

If you follow the Lord in your choice for a mate, you will make the right choice. That person will, in all actuality, be your soul mate because you've chosen a person that matches your character or your heart. There is nothing mystical about a soul mate but there is something very real about choosing someone who will *become* your soul mate forever.

The Ultimate Romance

"...Rachel was lovely in form and beautiful. Jacob was in love with Rachel and said, "I'll work for you seven years in return for your younger daughter Rachel."
Genesis 29:17-19

Have you ever been swept off your feet? Have you ever been given a gift that took your breath away? Maybe you have experienced the most romantic date in history or proudly displayed two dozen roses at work. Maybe you've been caught sitting at your desk and gazing into space, daydreaming of love. (Please tell me you haven't doodled Mr. and Mrs. So-and-so on your paper. Ok, I've done that too. Shhhhh, I won't tell if you won't!) The bottom line is this, romance is powerful.

When romance is expressed love is felt. Romance is the art of 'wooing' and pursuing, to be courted like in the good 'ole' days. 'Wooing', pursuing, and courting seem to be a history lesson that needs to be re-taught to most of us; it is a lesson worth learning and living.

The love story of Jacob and Rachel is an amazing one: it is a story of pursuit, perseverance, and undying love. Jacob began to work for his uncle Laban. Laban had recognized all the hard work and loyalty that Jacob had given him and offered to pay Jacob for his work. Jacob requested that no payment be made, only that he be granted the hand of his youngest daughter Rachel in marriage. Genesis 29:18 says, "Jacob was in love with Rachel and said, "I'll work for you seven years in return for your younger daughter Rachel." Wow, seven years of labor in order to marry Rachel. Talk about committed love! Talk about a lot of work! Jacob CHOSE to do this out of love and commitment to Rachel. Verse 20 says, "So Jacob served seven years to get Rachel, but they seemed like only a few days to him because of his love for her." I know, I know... how sweet! What a beautiful love story, right? Well it doesn't stop there. The seven years 'flew' by and it was time for the wedding. Laban tricked Jacob and had him marry his older daughter Leah instead; that is such a party foul! Jacob was obviously angered at the deceit but Laban agreed to allow him to marry Rachel...for another seven years of work...and he agreed! What this story demonstrates is that there is value to romance; there is value to wooing and chasing the love you desire. How do you think Rachel viewed Jacob? I can only imagine that she saw him as a hopeless romantic (present-day term of course!). Jacob was a man that saw her worth 14 years of labor and hard work; he was man who wanted her and was willing to wait and work for her hand in marriage. Wow. I'll say it again. Wow. That's impressive especially when our idea of romance is when the guy picks up the check for the burgers and fries! If you throw in a milkshake, you've got yourself a keeper! Jacob may not have used flowers, candy, or bought his girl a new car, but it was romance none-the-less because Jacob's intent for love was demonstrated through his actions.

Did you know that you are being pursued even now? Can you hear the love ballad playing in the background? Can you see the rose petals scattered on the floor and the smell of dinner on the table? You really are being pursued right now. Even as you read this line, you are being wooed and courted with the desire and intent for love. By whom, you might ask? Actually you might be grabbing a pen and paper to right down the address of where this romantic pursuit is happening - I don't blame you; I would be anxious and ready too!

The Lord says in Jeremiah 31:3, "I have loved you with an everlasting love; I have drawn you with loving kindness." How utterly romantic! Can you imagine ANYONE saying that to you? The amazing thing is it's not just anyone: it's the King of Kings. Psalm 45:11 says this, "The King is enthralled by your beauty." Has anyone ever been enthralled by your beauty? Not just your outward appearance, but you - who you are

The One

inside and outside. Enthralled, anyone, ever? God is. The Lord knows how to romance us. He invented it.

The Lord doesn't just 'romance us' and leave us to our own accord. There is no 'wining and dining' and then out the door He goes. There's more, much more. Sometimes love and romance take a sacrifice: in fact love is demonstrated most effectively when there is a sacrifice involved. The author, David Kenyon Webster, has said, "Those things which are precious are saved only by sacrifice." John 3:16 shares God's sacrifice for us: "For God so loved the world that he gave his one and only Son, that whoever believes in him will not perish but have eternal life." Romans 5:8 echoes this truth: "But God demonstrates his own love for us in this; while we were still sinners, Christ died for us."

God chose to put His romance for us into action, an action that is so difficult for me to even comprehend: He gave His Son for you and for me. Jesus Christ died so God could show just how much He loves you. God put His Son on a cross to die like a sinner instead of putting me there…or you. Jesus was the sacrificial Lamb so I wouldn't have to be; He died so I would not have to. That cross had my name on it… it had your name on it. Instead God crossed out my name and wrote Jesus' name there. All for the sake of pure love.

Let that sink in. Has anyone ever sacrificed so much for you in order to prove their love? Third Day wrote a song called *Just To Be With You* that captures this idea perfectly.

> I've heard a tale that a man would climb a mountain
> Just to be with the one he loves.
> How many times has he broken that promise?
> It has never been done
> Well I never climbed the highest mountain,
> but I walked the hill of calvary
> And just to be with you I'll do anything,
> there's no price I would not pay, no
> Just to be with you I will give everything.
> I would give my life away.
> And I know that you don't understand the fullness of my love
> How I died upon the Cross for your sin
> And I know that you don't realize how much that I give you
> And I promise I would do it all again

Back in the day of the knights, Sir Knight, as a final preparation for going to war, would gallantly trot to the princess who would give him a handkerchief. The handkerchief was not simply so Sir Knight could blow his nose or anything (that would be gross) but in order to signify that the princess was in love with the knight and she wanted him to come back from the battle. Is a handkerchief a real sacrifice? Uhmm… not really. Even if Grandmother Eunice had hand stitched it for a year it's still just a handkerchief. No real sacrifice was involved. How about a tattoo? Has anyone lovingly tattooed your name on their arm as a sign of love? First of all, I hope not…really. A tattoo might hurt for a little while but eventually the pain wears off and they have a permanent sign of their undying love for you…until you break up. Then he tattoos a motorcycle over your name. Not as romantic as you might think, huh? What I'm trying to say is that God did something extravagant to show love to you. He did something no ordinary person would do because He is no ordinary person. He is God and He is in love with you.

You can receive this love by receiving Christ as your own personal Savior. Romans 10:9 says, "That if you confess with your mouth, 'Jesus is Lord' and believe in your heart that God raised him from the dead, you will be saved." If you are tired of not being loved, not being wooed, not being pursued or desired then I'm asking you to do something radically different; something that will change your outlook on life and love forever; something that will make you feel eternally loved: receive Christ now and continue experiencing the Ultimate Romance.

To Find "The One" You Have to be "The One"

The wisest men follow their own direction
Euripides

Have you ever heard the phrase, 'Be the ball'? It's usually used in sports to help focus the athlete: it's a reminder to 'be' that which they are looking for in order to be successful. A baseball player would imagine that as the pitch was coming in at 93 miles an hour that he is the ball in order to concentrate on hitting the ball. Smack, a homerun! A golfer imagines that he is the golf ball as he taps it into the hole for a birdie. So to find your "One", you need to 'Be the ball'.

It's really easy to look for the 'right' person; it's harder to **be** the right person yourself. "You must be the change you wish to see in the world." Mahatma Gandhi. Gandhi is right: we need to take the time to possess the qualities that we may demand of another. The ironic part is that you can look everywhere for him or her, but if you are not the 'best you' they might pass YOU over. That would really stink, huh? Sometimes we can be so focused on the search for our mate we forget that **we** are someone's mate as well.

You might be asking, "So, how am I supposed to be 'The One'? Good question and I'm glad you asked. John Piper says, "Success in marriage is not finding the right person, but being the right person in the power of the one perfect Person." What are you looking for in a mate? What qualities must he or she have in order to win your heart? I challenge you to make a list of those qualities and characteristics that he or she needs to have in order to catch you. Then, and this is the hard part, YOU work on developing those qualities. Yes you! If these qualities are important for your mate to have then they are important enough for you to have as well. Please don't put the book down. I'm just challenging you to be who *you* expect someone else to be.

Below are some basic examples of what I'm talking about. Everyone has specific characteristics that they are looking for in their mate, but I want to share a few that are quite common. Remember these are qualities that you can develop in order to be the kind of person others are looking for. Please notice the order in which they are placed: it is not a coincidence. I believe that this should be the priority listing for all of us! So, are you ready to 'Be the Ball'?

Spirituality

Spirituality is the first quality we will discuss (remember I told you that I have placed them in order of importance - have you?) In your dreams of a husband/wife, you can see them helping you get the 'little ones' ready on Sunday morning for church. Maybe you desire for them to be an active member of a church, a deacon, a teacher, etc. You envision them praying before each meal an inspirational blessing. You know that when the kids are sick your mate will be right there laying hands on them and praying for them. You want your mate to be spiritual. Are you?

Many people want their mates to be Christians; they want their mates to have a meaningful and close relationship with the Lord. However they don't have that close walk themselves. Don't count on your mate to be the one who is strong spiritually: YOU be that one. The truth is <u>a strong Christian attracts a strong Christian</u>. I have heard on many occasions, "If he could just find a good Christian girl she could really help turn him around!" or "If she could just find a great Christian guy she would get into church." Here's the problem with that line of thinking: a strong Christian girl will not settle for a guy who is less than that. Not that he has to be perfect, but he has to be on HIS way to being a strong Christian on his own. When I met Lindsey he had been saved for about two years. He didn't have the entire Bible memorized and he, like all of us, still had his struggles. However what I saw in him was a passion to grow into the man God had created him to be: he was becoming like Christ and had a desire to do the will of God. I can honestly tell you this: I would not have considered one date with him (which would have been hard because he's a hottie!) if I felt like he wasn't strong and becoming stronger in his faith. I would *not* have made it my responsibility to 'date him into Christianity' or to use my strong relationship with the Lord to help him have one. He was a 'sold out Christian' who was looking for a 'sold out Christian'. That's how we found each other.

You need to develop your relationship with Christ: after you have accepted Him as your personal Savior, then you must grow spiritually. When you spend time reading God's Word, talking to Him, and listening to what He has to say to you, you become strong in your faith (and quite attractive to other Christians I might add).

I can tell you this: a Godly man is looking for a Godly woman and vice versa. Lindsey has said that once he got saved, the girls he once was attracted to were no longer the girls he was attracted to now. He was looking for something far greater than just a girl: he was looking for one who loved the Lord even more then she would ever love him. He was looking for a girl who exuded the love of Christ; a girl who stood up for her beliefs and didn't look like the rest of the world. He was looking for a girl who would be a Godly wife and even more importantly a Godly mother. What if *I* had been just some girl? Some girl who didn't have a relationship with Christ? Some girl who was more into the party scene that Jesus? Lindsey would have never chosen me: he would have never picked me, never asked me out, never fallen in love with me. Do you see how important it is to be strong spiritually? Make it a priority to grow strong in the Lord. Then, when you meet your Godly mate, you can encourage and strengthen EACH OTHER in your walks. Quit just looking for the one who loves the Lord and BE the one who loves the Lord!

Morality

You know I've never talked to anyone who has said they wanted their life mate to be a louse; I've never heard that they wanted their spouse to be immoral, a liar, a cheat, or a bum. Basically we all want to be with someone who is moral and has values. You don't want to marry a murderer or a thief, right? Well, how do you measure up?

I can pretty much guarantee that you are none of those mentioned (unless, of course, you are reading this from your cell. In that case, I apologize for the assumption but glad you are reading this!) But see morality goes much deeper than that. Personally I believe that the Bible lays out morality for us in black and white: it's called the Ten Commandments. Ever heard of them? There was a movie about them but I'd rather read about them in living color and without Charlton Heston. I won't share all ten of the Commandments, just a few which will help you define morality.

The First Commandment says "You shall have no other gods before me." The first question regarding your morality is, "Is God *your* God?" Is He number one in your life? To be a moral person He must be your God. It makes sense right? With no moral compass, which is God, how do you define morality? If God isn't yours how can you do the things He declares moral and stay away from the things He declares immoral? You can't and you don't. One of the problems with today's society is that since we have let go of God as the director of our morality, morality has become wishy-washy. It has become whatever a person wants it to be: no right, no wrong; just do what feels good and be true to yourself. If this is how you think you have just made yourself a 'god'. There *is* right; there *is* wrong. God has determined which is which a long time ago. He established it for us in order that we would live safe, productive, moral, and valued lives. So are you moral? The question is not do you conserve energy, save the planet, and recycle (not that those things are not important.) But more importantly, is God your God? If He is you have started this journey with the perfect compass: God.

The Third Commandment reads, "You shall not misuse the name of the Lord your God..." The King James Version (you know the one: "the-eth, thou-eth, those-eth" etc.) says, "Thou shalt not use the Lord's name in vain." The words that come from our mouth are a real testimony to our morality. Matthew 12:34 says, "...For out of the overflow of the heart the mouth speaks." Yikes! What is in our hearts will eventually find its way out of our mouth. I only have to spend a little time with someone to see in their heart. Am I a doctor? No, but in hearing their words I become privy to what is going on inside of them. Eventually people begin to speak what is actually in their heart: when I hear foul speech that reeks, I have seen what's in their hearts without the use of surgery. Whether it's cursing, using God's name in vain, or throwing His name around flippantly, the Third Commandment tells us to be careful of those who don't hold God's name in high esteem. How's your heart: stinky and smelly or moral and full of life?

The Ninth Commandment says "You shall not give false testimony." That simply means to lie. Did you know that your values and morals decide whether or not you lie? Do you lie about the 'small' things just not the big things? You know, little white lies, stories, exaggerations? A person who lives morally knows that a lie is a lie is a lie. Acts 5:4 says, "You have not lied to men but to God." Oops! You are probably saying, "I would never lie directly to God; are you kidding?" But, see, morality just isn't what others see in us: it's what God sees in us. Would you marry a person that bluntly tells you he/she would lie on their taxes? Probably not because you know what kind of repercussions that would cause for you and your family. Would you marry someone who has told you that committing murder really isn't a big deal? I would guess not since you might be the next victim, right? Let me ask you this: would you lie about your age? (I can say that because I'm still 29…okay, okay, just kidding…I'm 30. Oh boy! Hang on while I repent!) But do you get my drift? Would you give back too much change if a clerk messed up? Would you lie to a police officer about how fast you were going? "Ummm…I was going 35?" when you know you were going 65 in a 25? See how and when morality works? It works for the good of people and it *should* work all of the time.

Morality is essential to 'being the ball'. We want morality to cover our potential mate, but the thing is we need to be covering ourselves in morality as well. Being moral is not always easy. It is, however, always the right way to live; a Godly man/woman will recognize morality in our lives and know the impact that it makes. Our morals or values will define each life decision. Roy Disney says, "It's not hard to make decisions when you know what your values are." He's correct. If you struggle with some part of morality the moral compass, God, is willing and able to help you with it. It is His desire for all of us to have morals and values that reflect His heart for His people. Ask Him to help guide you in morality enjoying all of its freedom.

Sense of Family

You probably want your man/woman to have a strong sense of family: you want them to treat their parents with love, honor, and respect. Family must mean something to him/her because, if it all works out, you'd be his/her family too, right?

Family was important to me when it came to my future husband. I have had wonderful relationships with my boyfriend's family, but I've had rocky ones as well. I would watch and listen to how my boyfriends would talk to and about their moms especially; just a personal opinion here, but I think that tells a lot about how he'd treat you. Anyway it was important to me that my husband-to-be loved his family. While I was going through my time of singleness with the Lord, I began to realize that *I* had a lot of work to do in the area of my own family: there was mending, forgiving, and loving to be done. I realized that I had to begin nurturing the very relationships that had once nurtured me.

I'm very excited to tell you that because of the hard work that went in to repairing, renewing, and refreshing my relationship with my family my parents are now our closest friends. If you would have asked me when I was sixteen if I would even like my parents ten years later let alone consider them my best friends, I probably would have peed myself from all the laughing. But as God would have it Lindsey even benefits from my relationship-building efforts. He sees my parents as his own and I utterly adore that. It would have never happened unless I made my family relationship as important to me as I wanted my spouse's to be to him. Something interesting to think about, isn't it?

So here's what I'm thinking: a lot of you have some work to do in the area of your family: estranged parents that maybe you have written off simply because they've told you things you didn't want to hear or siblings you have 'issues' with. It is time to repair and mend those broken relationships. Not only is it good for you to do in general but you are also making your life better for when you do find "The One". You won't have to make up stories of why you and your family aren't so close anymore; you won't have to dread taking him/her to meet your family (if, of course, you've chosen the right him or her). Basically you are doing this to better your life now as well as your spouse's life later. Romans 12:19 says, "If it is possible, as far as it depends on you, live at peace with everyone." Do everything in your power to repair, renew, refresh, and reignite your family relationships. If you've done your part and it is still un-repairable, then focus your energy on the family relationships that are healthy. Your spouse will thank you and you will reap huge benefits as well!

Financial Freedom

As far as financial freedom goes I'm not talking about wealth. I'm not saying that it wouldn't be nice to marry a rich chic or dude. I'm just saying that it's not the amount of money you have; it's what you do with that money. For women we like to know that we are secure especially financially. We want to know that our needs are, and will be, met in that area. So it makes sense that if you want financial freedom and security in your partner, YOU must be financially secure as well.

We all will struggle financially at one time or another in our lives. I remember that during my first year of teaching I made $1500 dollars a month. I know: don't laugh so hard! That money had to stretch to pay my rent, car, insurance, student loans, groceries, tithe, phone, electric, water, etc. As you can imagine, there was very little left. I had to be so wise with my money or I wouldn't be able to survive. Did I eat out? Nope. Did I spend frivolously? Nope. Did I waste gas money? Nope. I worked the after-school program to earn money; I even babysat just to get ahead. I had to choose to be wise in my spending. You know what? I never missed a payment, never ran out of money, and never had to ask anyone to bail me out with a loan. God is faithful, friend, and He is in the business of taking care of MY business! I remember one time I received $20 dollars in the mail from an anonymous person. The note read, "God wanted me to give this to you." I was so excited about that $20 dollars and used it to buy what I needed…gas and tampons. What? It's what I needed at the time and I was so very thankful that God cared enough about me needing tampons that He provided them for me… talk about a God of details!

I think the most important thing to remember about money is that it's not ours to begin with. The Lord is the reason we have anything and we are to give back just a small portion of what He so greatly blessed us with. It's called tithing and it's so very important to the life of a believer. As you are trying to 'be the ball', you should be tithing as you would want your spouse-to-be to tithe as well. A great benefit is that when you get married to "The One" he or she has already established the discipline of tithing; it's a done deal, a habit, something that is as natural as breathing.

Another important aspect to remember about money: it truly is about disciplining yourself to spend wisely. Whether you are the primary money-maker or not it is imperative to make the money you have stretch as far as it possibly can. Before I was married I handled all my money best way I could; I felt the need and desire to spend only when necessary and stretch my pennies as far as they'd reach. This was great preparation for being a wife, mother, and a part-time money maker in our family. I've known young women who max out their credit cards and have hefty debt before marriage. Not only is it a travesty to bring all that debt into marriage, it displays the lack of financial foresight that is needed in marriage. I've known young men to pour a huge amount of money into their hobbies (video games, accessorizing the car, hunting, etc) and have little money left for anything else. What they *will* realize is that when they are married hobbies do have their place, but their place is not to deplete the bank! Statistics show that the majority of marriages that end in divorce cite 'money problems' as the number one reason for divorce. It is necessary that you go into a relationship already understanding the importance of wisdom in the area of money. With that you will be bringing into your relationship more value than a dollar could ever hold.

Submission to Authority

Did you just roll your eyes? I think you may have! Hear me out on this and then afterwards, you can roll your eyes all you want…just don't let my dad see it…he hates that.

Here's what I mean by authority: a boss, a parent, a teacher, someone in leadership, etc. You should be looking for someone who respects authority. Why you might ask? Well if he/she doesn't answer to someone he/she will **live** like they don't have to answer to anyone. Therein lies the trouble. When we are not accountable, nothing matters: not the choices we make, not the consequences we could face. Nothing. Look at

The One

this idea another way: if a guy/girl cannot accept authority then he/she will probably not surrender to the authority of God. Romans 13:2 says, "Consequently, he who rebels against the authority is rebelling against what God has instituted and those who do so will bring judgment on themselves."

If you want to 'be the ball', you will have to submit to authority in your life. The obvious and most important is to the Lord. When a person surrenders his/her will to the Lord and says, "God, whatever you want me to do, I will do it. I may not want to or even like it, but if you say it, I'm on board," what they have done is recognize God's authority in their life. They've submitted to His will and His way as opposed to doing it their way. For some this is easy; for others this is torture. Take me, for example. I was very independent and strong-willed (remember what my brother said to Lindsey earlier?). I wanted things my way and I wanted to do them myself. As a little girl I would use phrases like "No, I do it by myself!" or with my arms crossed and chin up "You're not the boss of me!" Okay, who am I kidding really? I still say those things sometimes! There were definite moments growing up where my parents and I would have 'intense moments of communication' (okay, that actually means arguments!): the majority of those moments were caused by the fact that I did not want to submit to their authority. It may have been over something I was wearing, somewhere I was going, or someone I was seeing. They used their God-given authority to help steer me in the right direction. If I had been wiser I would have listened and respected that direction instead of rebelling against it.

I have definitely grown in the area of submitting to authority. I think I just heard my mom and dad yell, "Well, praise the LORD!" The difference was I knew that if I wanted a man to surrender under the perfect authority of God I would have to do the same. Here's the thing though: God is good. Jeremiah 29:11 says that His plans for me are full of hope and a future. So I have to believe that surrendering and submitting to Him is the one way to be sure that I get that hope and future.

Here are some warning signs for someone who does not respect or submit to authority:
- If he/she talks badly about their parents in the realm of their authority: "They are always on my back about coming

home on time or not spending so much time on the phone. I don't care what they say; I'll do what I want when I want." Hello red flag.
- If he/she tells you that they don't have to answer to anyone because they are their own boss. Run away...run fast. You don't want anyone who thinks 'they' are the boss; what this really means is that they will always look out for themselves, never lay down their life for you, and never think of you first. I can tell you something...you will be miserable... forever...or until he/she is tired of you.
- If he/she is continuously in trouble with the law. You have just stumbled on someone with an authority issue. When they make choices based on the belief that the law does not apply to them then their decisions will continue to be poor. You DO NOT want to be a part of those poor decisions, now or in the future.

Be the person who lives under the authority of Christ and of those He chooses to put above you: your boss, your parents, your government, etc. As you surrender your authority to that of the Lord you will actually be stronger than you've ever been. Anyone can be their own boss, but it takes someone extraordinary to allow God to be in control of their life. Trust me. This comes from the girl who, if put in the corner and told to sit down, would say to herself, "Self, I might be sitting on the outside but I'm standing up on the inside." Miracles do happen. Ask God.

Confidence

Now, notice I did NOT say cockiness; I said confidence. There is a HUGE difference. Ask Dennis Rodman: he'll tell you. Cockiness is defined as being over-confident or arrogantly confident and sure of yourself. It's not very attractive: it's like putting on your most beautiful outfit and then rolling around in mud. Confidence is the ability to accept one's personal strengths and weaknesses. It is the ability to be secure in those strengths yet willing to work on the weaknesses as well. Most people are naturally attracted to confidence: when we find someone who has confidence in himself/herself we are attracted to that

The One

confidence…and usually attracted to him/her as well! In order to 'be the ball' as we've been discussing you must have confidence.

So, how do you have confidence? And in what should you have confidence? The better question is in *whom* should we have confidence? If you were to ask my friends and family if I was a confident person they would answer yes: I know because I've asked them. See, I am a very confident person. Do you know why? Because I know that I'm dirty, nasty, filthy, gross, disgusting, selfish, relentless, pathetic, and downright evil. You are probably thinking, "Ummm…I think she missed out on what confidence really is." No. Actually I figured out WHO it is. I am nothing, but because I am the Lord's and He is mine, I am something. Not only that I am something beautiful.

Confidence radiates from those who have figured out that they are nothing without the Lord: we can't take our next breath without Him. Psalm 71:5 says, "For you have been my hope, O Sovereign Lord, my confidence since my youth." I can be confident not in me but in Him.

If you want to capture your "One" who is confident then you must be confident as well. Be confident not of your abilities, capabilities, gifts, or talents but of the One who made you that way. Be confident of the fact that the Lord Jesus Christ loves you and that He laid down His life for you. Be confident that you are fearfully and wonderfully made; know that He calls you by name and has a future for you. Be positive of the fact that without Him you'd drown but with Him you'll soar. Stand firm in the knowledge that you are the apple of His eye and He holds you purposefully in the palm of His hand. Do you get the drift? Your confidence will attract those who are confident. Yet beware and remember that cockiness could be just around the corner from confidence. Cockiness is an arrogant reliance on self and confidence is a humble reliance on God. Proverbs 3:34 says, "God opposes the proud but gives grace to the humble". I am confident because I am nothing and He is everything. See how attractive that is?

So 'being the ball' seems to be quite a chore, but it is a chore worth working toward. No one will be perfect at all of these: trust me; I've looked. But what you want is someone **striving** for that perfection. Paul writes in 2 Corinthians 13:11 to "aim for perfection". Neither you nor your "One" may actually be perfect in these qualities but love your future mate enough to aim for it. You may come closer than you think!

While I am Waiting…

So, I was just thinking about how people say they are 'waiting' for their mate. After reading how we should be **actively pursuing** the character traits in ourselves that we want the "One" to have I have come to the conclusion that there is really not much 'waiting' involved. Instead there's a lot of 'working' going on. If these character traits are important for your mate to have then they are certainly important enough for you to be pursuing as well: take the necessary time to craft your character into the kind of person you want to be. At this moment in time are you the person you want to be? Are you the person that you've hoped you would become? This is your chance. You don't have to wait to become your best. Begin now knowing that as you mold and form your character into something worthwhile, somebody, somewhere is doing the same. Maybe it will make the time go by so much faster. Work on being "The One" not just waiting for "The One". And in the meantime enjoy the person you will become!

You're Worth the Wait

But the important thing about learning to wait, I feel sure, is to know what you are waiting for.
Anna Neagle

Do you like cake? What? It's a legitimate question. Do you like cake: any cake, a specific kind of cake, certain icing? I love me some cake! My husband has said that he has never seen me pass up a piece of cake. He's right: I wouldn't want to hurt anyone's feelings; I'm just being polite.

It doesn't just stop at loving cake. I love cupcakes, cookies, pies… did I tell you I work out a lot? I have to. Because I love to eat cake it also means that I bake cakes too. I'll warn you in advance: I didn't say they were pretty; I just said that I baked them. One time I made a baseball cake for my son's first birthday. It was a round cake: by that I mean it was *supposed* to be round. It turned out slightly, well, not so round. It was tasty though. Have I mentioned that I love me some cake? Yeah, I thought I might have.

As much as I love eating cake the hardest part is the baking of the cake. It takes time to prepare it, bake it, and then clean up after it (boy do I make a mess!). Let's just take a minute to go through the process of baking a cake. First, you have to make sure you have all the ingredients to make the cake. When I make it typically I have help from one Betty Crocker. I mean, why fight it? She did all the work already…let her.

So, prep- wise for me it means getting out the box, the eggs, the oil, and water. Then you mix it all together in the mixing bowl. I recently got one of the mixers that are hands free: love those things! Not that I actually do anything else but watch the beater stir: it just makes me feel like I *could* walk away if I wanted to. Anyway the mixer agitates all the ingredients together to form a batter (don't forget: you have to take the time to scrape the bowl so the batter doesn't stay on the sides). Then you pour the cake batter into the cake pans that you have already sprayed and floured. You stick the pans in the oven and wait. And wait. And, well, wait some more. I hate waiting because I love me some cake: just writing about makes me crazy. I just drooled on the keyboard. Let me ask you something: what would happen if I were to pull out the cakes after they had been in the oven for 10 minutes? Duh…it wouldn't be ready. Okay, say 15 minutes? Still not ready. How about 25 minutes? Well it's closer but it still needs to be in the oven for 32-37 minutes in order for it to be done, right? Right. If I pull it out too early it will be like a story my dad told about his mom, my nanny (who was, by the way, a real spitfire: there is some resemblance I admit) who had made them a cake. She baked it and put it on the table for the four kids. My dad said they sliced it and began eating it. Enthusiastically they asked, "Hey mom, how did you get the pudding in the middle of the cake?" Nanny groaned and replied, "There's no pudding in the cake…" (I think it got thrown away, but honestly I think my dad would have eaten it anyway…he loves cake too, it's genetic.) Unless we wait the necessary time to bake the cake we get a cake that's not ready. It's not that it's totally disgusting; it's just that it has not reached its full potential. It's not all it is supposed to be. However, when you wait the 32-37 minutes for the cake to bake and pull it out, wait for it to cool, ice it, and then cut into it…yowzer it's good! And you think to yourself, "Self, that was worth the wait". So are you.

So is the person you will be waiting for. We can look at it from two angles. The first is that you, friend, are worth the time it takes to get you; the second is that your "One" needs to be ready also, not mushy on the inside like my Nanny's cake. Let's see why you are worth the wait.

I think about all the necessary steps to get a cake ready to be edible, everything from the correct ingredients to adding the eggs one at a time (that really does make a difference!). I think about how the mixer had to agitate those ingredients together in order to make something tasty. Have you ever just tasted the cake flour by itself? How about just swallowing a whole egg? Ever chug some vegetable oil? Doesn't sound real tasty, does it? I can assure you: it would not taste like a cake. All of the ingredients together are what forms a cake; without those specific ingredients the cake would not taste like a cake. Extract the eggs and your cake is heavy and gross. Forget the oil and you've just made a dessert fit for the birds (who, by the way, would probably turn their beaks up at it!). Those combined ingredients, the ones that were agitated and stirred up, are what make the cake so good.

Your life has been a set of ingredients: a little hope, a few dashes of disappointment, a bottle of joy, and a dollop of perseverance. It has made you who you are. The agitation of life has mixed those ingredients into something worthy. If you rush through your life just to get a mate, then you may have skipped some very important and vital ingredients to your life. Your waiting assures that your ingredients (your life) will be complete. Why would you want to rush the process that will prepare you for the person you are waiting for?

I can speak from experience, and I can speak loudly! I remember, after my breakup, I wondered 'when': when will I meet him; when will we get married; when, when, when! I now humbly realize that I wouldn't have wanted to get married any sooner than I did or with any other man than I did. I've already shared how my heartbreak led to a search, and the search led to healing, growth, passion, fire, and wholeness in the Lord. I would not have wanted to have gotten married before all of those life ingredients had been stirred into my life. I wouldn't have been ready: I, dear one, would have been the cake with the pudding in the middle. Philippians 1:6 says, "...being confident of this, that he who began a good work in you will carry it on to completion until the day of Christ Jesus." You are also worth the wait. So, slow down, enjoy the ride, and experience the sensation of being "mixed" and "stirred" into the person that will one day be completed, icing and all!

This cake analogy applies to your future mate as well: you do not want to take your mate out of the oven before his/her time. Just like you don't want to rush your ingredients you do not want him/her until he or she are ready as well. You may not remember but earlier in the book I briefly mentioned how I had met Lindsey about five months earlier at a church crusade. It was the first time I had ever laid eyes on him. He introduced himself and we chatted a few minutes; actually, he said that I did all talking: he just listened. He was probably right. He shared with me many years later that he had wanted to ask me on a date but didn't. I was glad. You know why? Because we weren't cakes yet: I wasn't ready and neither was he. I was still experiencing the ingredients of heartbreak and sorrow; I was still being stirred into healing and wholeness. Lindsey would tell you that he wouldn't have been ready either: God was still tweaking areas of his life so that he could be a part of mine. You don't want them when they are not ready. You will not get their full potential, but instead you will receive a half baked cake: not horrific, just not the best it could be. Just like you are worth the wait so is he (or she). Allow God to do all that He desires to in each of you. When the timer goes off you will see that the solitary ingredients have made for you both: a cake worth eating.

The Past has Passed

The brightest future will always be based on a forgotten past, you can't go on well in life until you let go of your past failures and heartaches. -Unknown

How many times have you thought about mistakes you've made in the past? A million maybe? More? One thing most of us have in common is that we all have made mistakes in our past: some have made 'big' mistakes, some 'little', but mistakes none-the-less. With the memories of our mistakes, stupid decisions, and dumb choices come certain emotions or feelings: shame, regret, remorse, embarrassment, and frustration just to name a few. I don't think you will ever meet someone who will say, "I have never made a wrong decision in my past. I have no regrets on any of the choices I've made ever." If you meet that person, let me know: I'd like to give them some of mine.

The bottom line is that we've all messed up. We've all in some way, shape, or form, made a poor choice. It could have been with money, a relationship, a job, a spur-of-the-moment decision, a friendship, a night, a place…there are so many to choose from. The thing about poor choices from the past is that we can't change them; notice I didn't say we couldn't learn from them. In fact if we don't learn from them we are considered like a dog who returns to his puke (Proverbs 26:11)…sounds yummy, huh? But we don't have a time machine in order to fix those mistakes. If I did have a time machine I'd go back to the 80's: I had some really big hair I needed to change. So, what do we do with those failures, mess-ups, and completely screwed up choices?

Forget about them. No seriously: forget about them. Isaiah 43:18 says "Forget the former things, do not dwell on the past." We really do need to forget the former things: the things that we are not proud of; the things we would never choose to do again; the things that make us wish we could go back and call a 'do-over' or a 'take back' like in <u>Good Will Hunting</u>. The Bible clearly states to forget them and do not dwell on them. To dwell means to reside, stay, have your home, inhabit, and settle. So, what God is telling you, dear one, is don't <u>reside</u> in your mess-ups. Don't <u>stay</u> in the place of your memories that recall your wrongs. Don't <u>inhabit</u> or <u>make your home</u> in your poor choices. Choose not to <u>settle</u> in where your mistakes were made. So, I guess the next natural question would be WHY would we want to reside, stay, inhabit, have our home, or settle in our past?

I think one reason we dwell on our past is that we are really good at being our own worst critics. We know ourselves better than anyone (except God of course), and I think we are very critical of our wrongdoings. Why? If we are hard on ourselves it's not so bad if others are hard on us; if we've already been critical of our mess-ups when someone so 'kindly' points them out to us, we feel we can handle it better. We tend to punish ourselves over and over for mistakes we've made. Being our own worst critics can help us by driving us to make the right decision and choosing wisely, but it can also leave us feeling defeated, beat-up, resigned to failure, and overall like a bad person. I can tell you, beloved, this is NOT where God wants you to be. You are His, called by His name, and He loves you. If He chooses to forget your sins how about trying it for yourself? Hmmm…it could just work.

Another reason we dwell on our past is because it is a comfortable place for some of us. We partied hard and had a lot of fun, but we also did some really stupid things. We are comfortable with stupid. We feel like our past is so much a part of us that we feel the need to re-visit there often. Remembering: remembering easier times, fun times, or maybe not remembering so much. For some reason the past has this perpetual pull on us, calling us, and wooing us to think back: propelling us backward into time. Believe it or not this is an age old struggle. There is even a story about it in the Old Testament (it's the beginning part of the Bible…you should read it sometime – you just have to get through who "begot" whom).

The One

The book of Exodus tells of how God freed the Israelites from the slavery and oppression of Pharaoh in Egypt. These people were made to be slaves, tortured, and abused; they were nothing more than workhorses in a constant state of labor. Through many miracles God freed His people because of His great love for them. They were finally free from their past, finally free from the slavery and torture. Finally...free... free. How ecstatic do you think those Israelites were? How pumped would you have been? Their reaction was, well, stinky, to say the least. They had been in the desert on their way to what God had called the Promised Land, and God had been serving up miracles like a waitress at the Waffle House...impeccably. Are you ready for their reaction? In the desert the whole community grumbled against Moses and Aaron. The Israelites said to them, "If only we had died by the Lord's hand in Egypt! There we sat around pots of meat and ate all the food we wanted, but you have brought us out into this desert to starve this entire assembly to death." (Exodus 16:2-3) And again, 'They said, "Why did you bring us up out of Egypt to make us and our children and livestock die of thirst?" (Exodus 17:3) Can you believe them? They were delivered out of a situation that was horrible yet they WANTED to go back! Why? Because it was comfortable: they were more comfortable living in the past than facing their future. Sound familiar? It did for me too. There were times in my life that I would have much rather gone back to Egypt, where I was a slave, then to move forward to the Promised Land because I didn't really know what the Promised Land held. I knew what my past held, and as bad as it was, at least I knew.

It may be somewhat of a struggle, but we must, MUST, move ahead, comfortable or not. Philippians 3:13 says, "Forgetting what is behind and straining toward what is ahead, I press on..." Have you ever strained something before: maybe your neck, back, hamstring, or quad? It's hard to move forward after you've strained something; it takes work. It may be the same with you: you may actually have to **strain** toward what is ahead for you instead of dwelling on the past. Easier doesn't mean better. Would the Israelites have been better off staying in Egypt? Umm...that would be a NO, but they wanted to anyway. Forget what was. Strain towards what will be.

Why should we forget about the past and press on toward the Promised Land? Blessings, my friend, pure blessings! One of those blessings is found in Isaiah 43:19 (right after it tells us to forget the former things and not to dwell on the past): "See, I am doing a new thing!" Praise the Lord for new things! After we've messed up, dated the wrong guy, spent too much money, spoiled that relationship, or said the wrong thing, one thing we need is to be promised "a new thing".

The Promised Land was said to be full of milk and honey which was a sign of good things, promise, and favor. Do you know what we get when we forget what is behind? We receive God's good things, His promise, and His favor. I've met so many people who just want to go back to Egypt instead of moving towards the Promised Land. God describes that future in Jeremiah 29:11: "I know what I'm doing, I have it all planned out –plans to take care of you, not abandon you, plans to give you the future you hope for." (The Message) You might want to read that again; let it really sink in. God has the Promised Land all ready for us; we just have to 'go towards the light' so to speak. We must quit looking behind at the past and press on toward the future, a future that is full of hope and promise. I've heard the following comparison and thought it to be quite valid and useful. Think about your windshield. Think about how big it is and how much of the road ahead you can see. Now, think about your rearview mirror. See how small it is in comparison to the windshield? Why? Well, the purpose of the windshield is to see what lies ahead. The purpose of the rearview mirror is to see what is behind. Get my drift? If what was behind us was as important as what is ahead, the rearview mirror would be larger, much larger. But that is not the case. That thought helps put it all in perspective; at least it did for me. We need to be looking forward out of our windshield to our hopes, dreams, and future… Let the rearview take care of what has already passed.

This is NOT the Last Chapter...

You're writing the story of your life one moment at a time.
Doc Childre and Howard Martin

...of my book, yes, of your story...no. I'm not saying that I expect you to sit down and write a book (though, I have to admit, it's been fun!). I'm saying that you have a story. It is a story with many chapters. Some have already been written; some are waiting to be penned.

I've learned that when the Lord teaches me something in my life it is not only for my good: it is for my best. It shapes my character, refines my spirit, and sets my feet on the best path for my life. The question I had to ask myself is this, "Do I want a good life OR do I want the BEST life?" Not a tough question when you get right down to it! My life story was mapped out for my best. Sometimes the chapters in my life felt like they would never end. Sometimes they felt like they didn't last long enough. Regardless of the length each chapter was written on my heart because my Father loved me and desired what was considered "His Best".

As each chapter evolves in my life the titles may all be different but there is always one constant: God is faithful. Always. Everyday. Whether it was concerning a job, a relationship, or even the search for my husband...God is faithful. Faithful in providing, faithful in protecting; faithful to His promises. Psalm 145:13 "The LORD is faithful to all his promises and loving toward all he has made." He made me; therefore, He was faithful and loving: He's a God who is faithful far beyond what any man could ever be.

I had to set myself on a journey in search for true love. I was searching for someone to complete me, to know me fully yet love me anyway. I was desperately seeking a promise of forever, not just a contract of marriage, but a covenant of love. If you had asked me exactly what I was looking for I would have easily said, "Why, a husband of course!" I got one, dear friend. Isaiah 54:5 says, "Your husband is your maker, the Lord God almighty is His name." Christ is all I've ever needed; all the rest is just 'gravy'.

What does that mean for your story? It will be whatever you choose for it to be. You might be in the same place I was a few years ago: searching for your 'soul-mate' and waiting to find "The One." My prayer is that you would allow the Lord to speak what is best for you and then follow in that way. Beloved, I want to tell you something: it doesn't matter if you get married to someone if it's not the *right* one. This search is not something you can handle on your own; trust me: I tried and failed miserably. I've also counseled so many women (and by counseling I mean listening to them sob and handing them boxes of tissues) who are in the midst of divorce or in the middle of horrible relationships. Do you know what I want to tell them and often do? Did you pray about this choice? Did you seek Godly advice about this person? Was he a Christian when you met and married? Sadly the answers are often a resounding 'no'. And most often this realization comes way too late: the damage is done, the heart already broken, and a marriage dissolved. Unfortunately we live in the land of the walking wounded, wearing our battle scars on our hearts – or what's left of them anyway.

This grieves my spirit so. There are all of these precious people wandering around earth who pray for their meals and what kind of car to drive; yet, they don't even give the same thought to preparing for their mate. They don't spend time on their knees asking God, who knows what's best for them, what HE thinks. They forfeit the opportunity of knowing which way to go. Isaiah 30:21 says "Whether you turn to the right or to the left, your ears will hear a voice behind you saying, "This is the way, walk in it."

Don't you want to know which way to go, dear one? Don't you want to know that your choice of a husband or wife is the right one? Well, He

The One

wants you to know that too! God is not trying to hide His 'best' from you. He does not desire for you to wander in the wilderness for 40 years not knowing where He wants you to go. In fact He is ready and waiting for you to ask Him. So ask Him. He's easily found. Jeremiah 29:12-14a "Then you will call upon me and come and pray to me, and I will listen to you. You will seek me and find me when you seek me with all your heart. I will be found by you, declares the LORD."

If you are currently on this journey I ask that you would prayerfully consider all that you have read and ask the Lord to help you glean that which will benefit you. Ask your Creator to remind you of things you need to know in your search. Pray that He would cause your spirit to stir as you come across something that just may change your perspective, which in turn, could change your life.

Maybe you've already been down this road and found "The One". You've experienced the fullness of God's best in your mate and are now living in His abundance. This book hasn't really been a "learning experience" for you, just a really fun read (or at least I hope it was a fun read!). Would you ask God to put someone on your heart who needs this insight and then commit to praying for them diligently? Maybe it's a friends' son or daughter…maybe it's yours. It could be a friend of yours who you know is struggling through this journey called dating. It could possibly be a co-worker who recently got divorced and has been thrust back into the dating world after many years. I guess I'm just asking that you use this opportunity to minister to someone who is in need. Someone who will benefit from your prayers and just maybe this book. I may not be able to thank you in person, but please consider this my personal "thank you" for investing in that one person. You just never know how God may work…and to think, He chooses to use us to do so!

Oh, dear one, please remember that your Savior loves you more than any man or woman could ever even think about loving you. He is walking this journey along with you. My defining moment was when I realized that the One person I'd always wanted had never even left my side: He was and is my Abba, my Daddy. Honestly if I had never gotten married I would have lived. However I am certain that if I had not intimately and soulfully found my Heavenly Father I would have surely died.

So, I give you my best on your search for "The One". I have a feeling He's closer than you think.

Notes

Notes

Notes

Notes

Notes

Notes

Notes

Notes

Notes

Notes